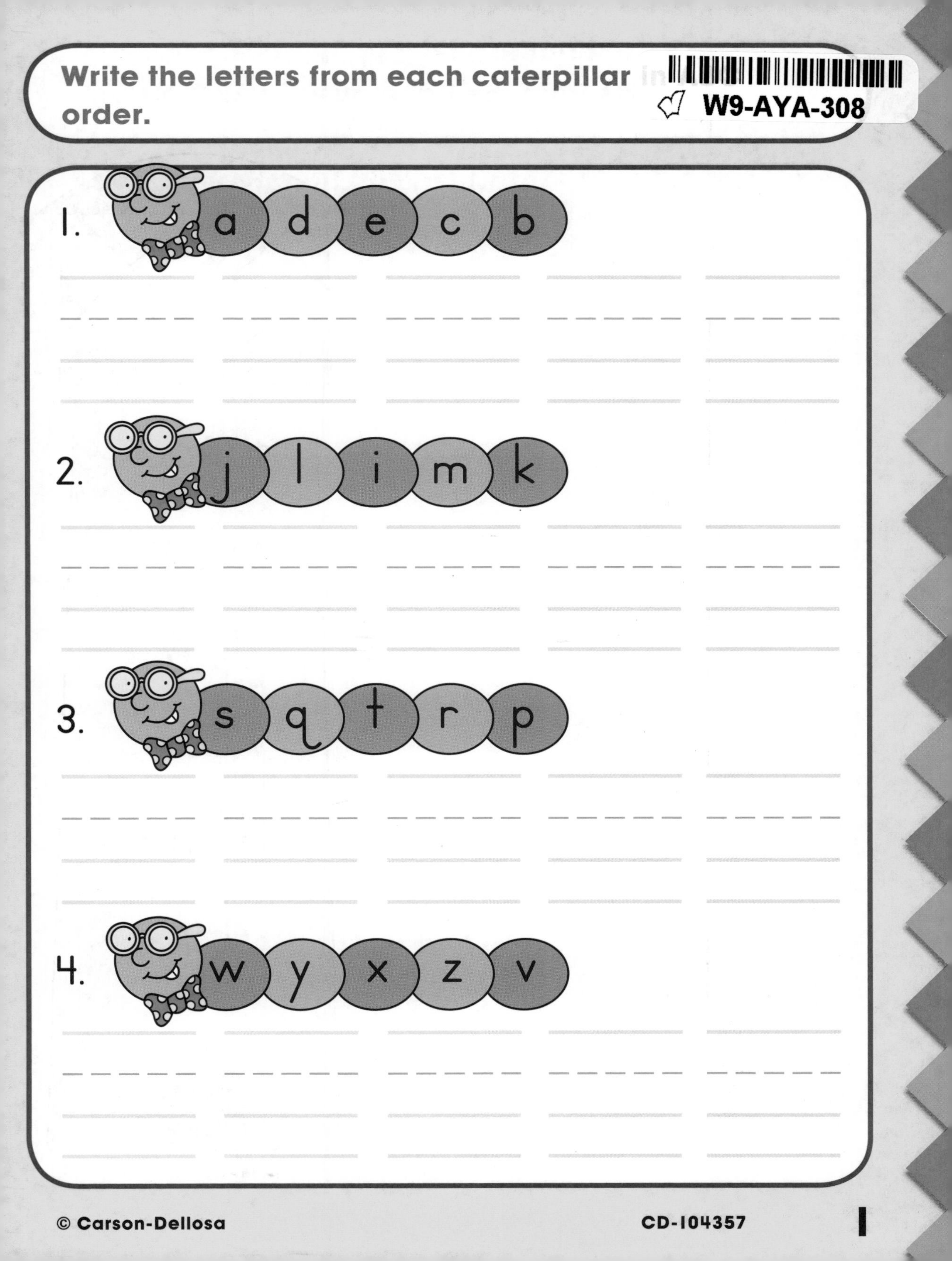

Write the letters from each caterpillar in ... order.

1. a d e c b

2. j l i m k

3. s q t r p

4. w y x z v

Write the words from the lighthouse in ABC order.

school

house

boy

car

friend

girl

Write the words from the lighthouse in ABC order.

jump

play

day

zoo

animal

look

Say the name of each picture. Write the letter of the beginning sound to complete the name.

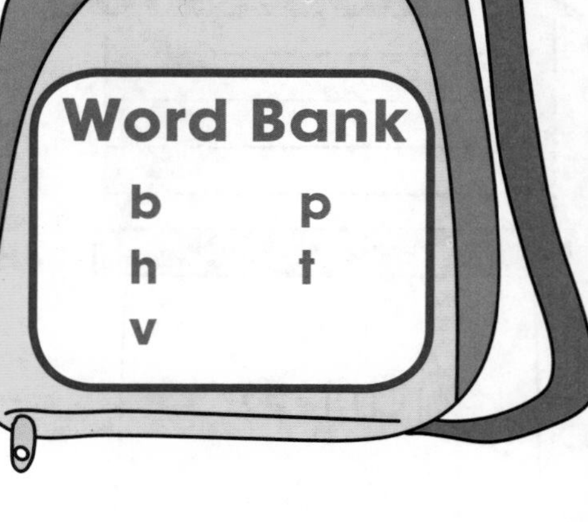
Word Bank
b p
h t
v

_____an

_____at

$25.00

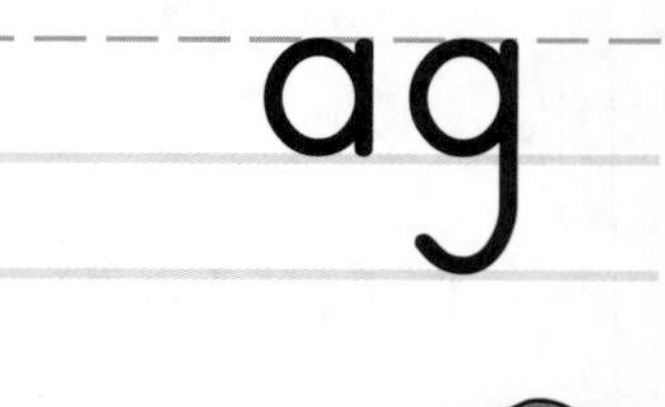

_____ag

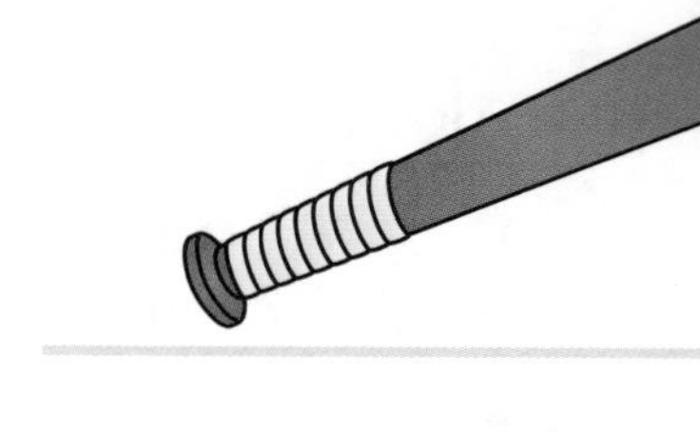

_____an

_____at

Write the correct word from the word bank to complete each sentence.

Word Bank

can fan ham map sad

1. I like to eat ____________.

2. She opened the ____________.

3. The girl is ____________.

4. We have a ____________.

5. The ____________ is not working.

Write words that rhyme with hat. Add letters from the hat to the -at ending.

Write words that rhyme with **pan**. Add letters from the pan to the **-an** ending.

Circle the words hidden in the puzzle. Words can be found across and down.

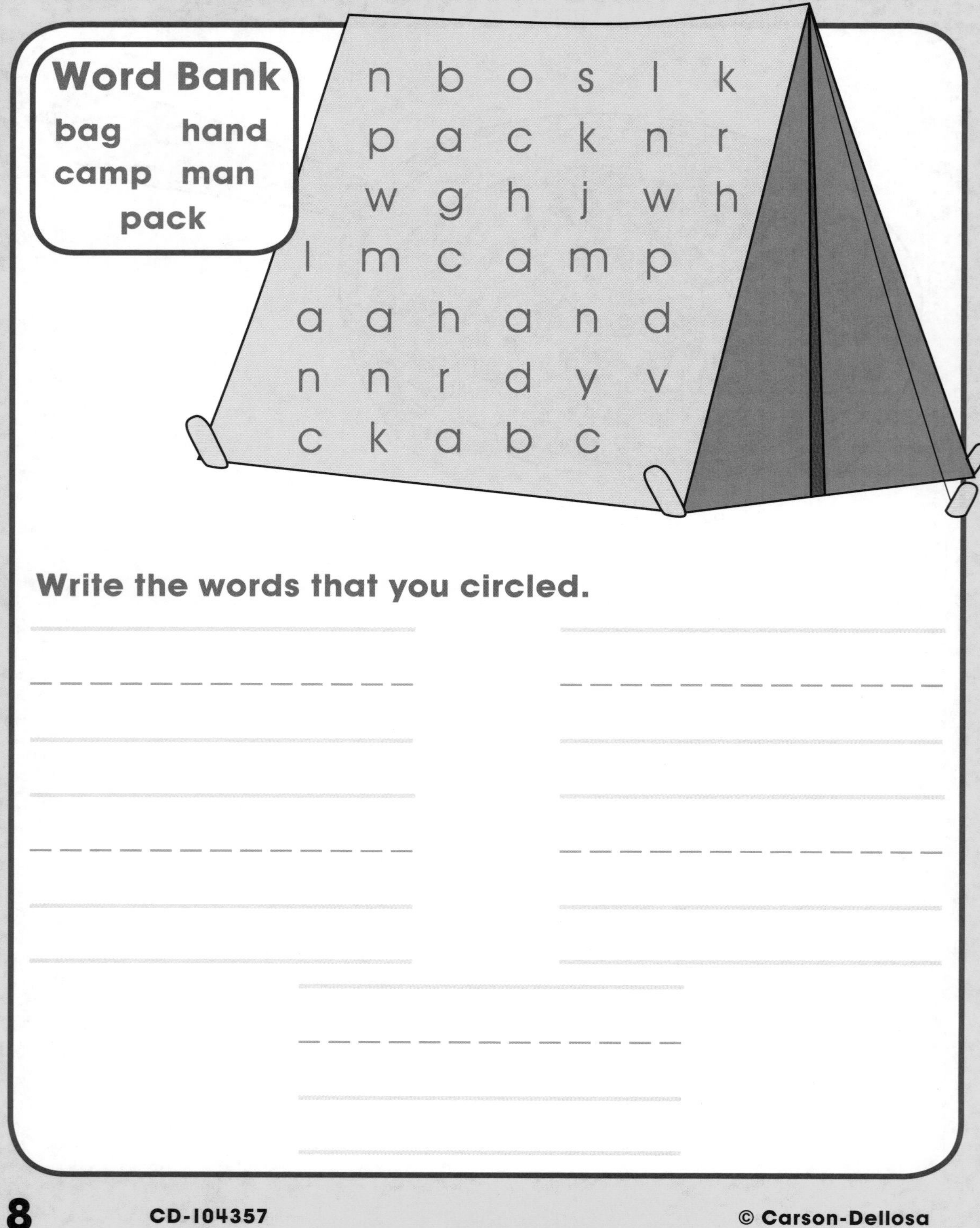

Write the words that you circled.

Say the name of each picture. Write the missing letter to complete each word.
beg
b g
b g
b g

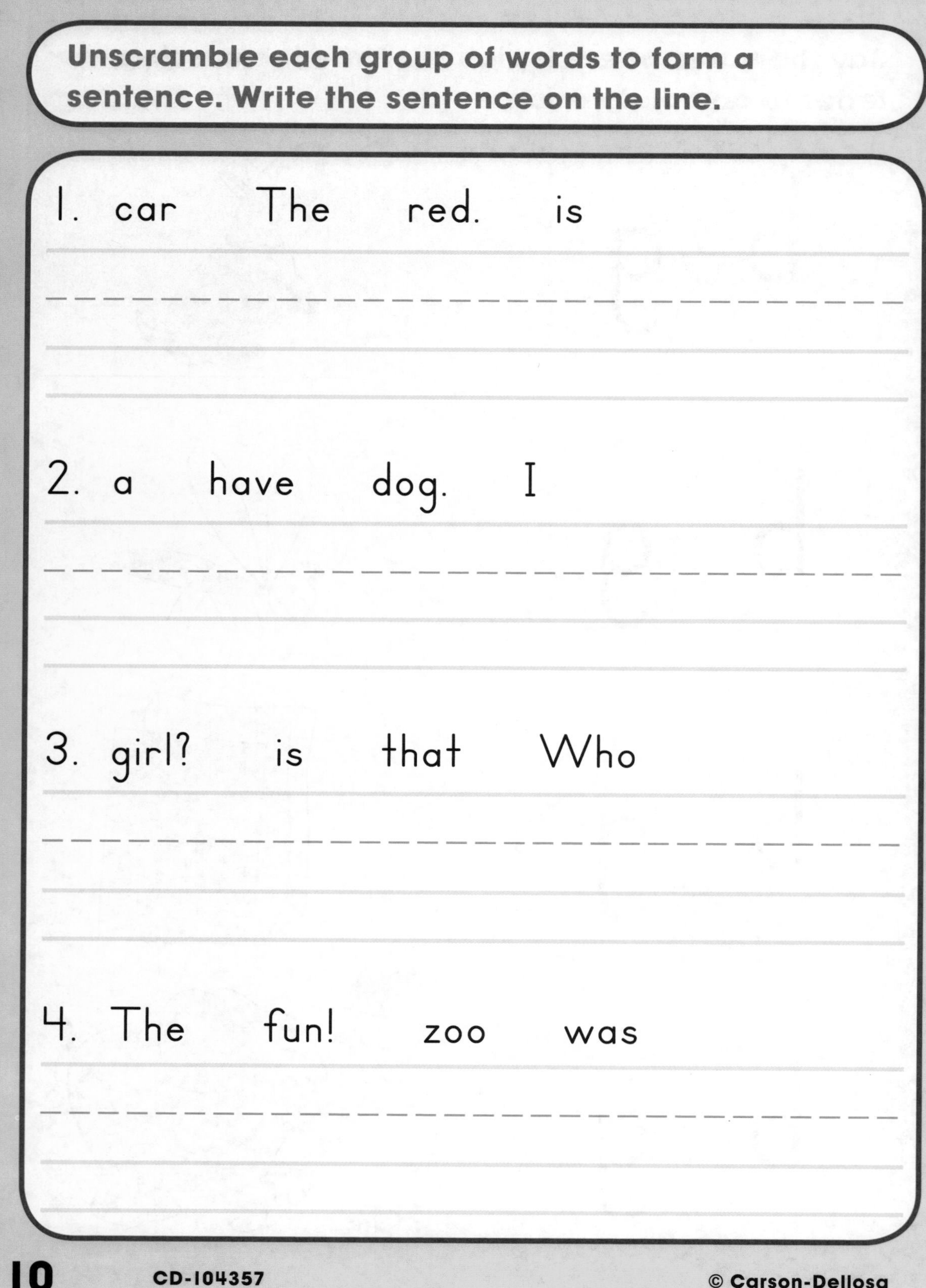

Unscramble each group of words to form a sentence. Write the sentence on the line.

1. car The red. is

2. a have dog. I

3. girl? is that Who

4. The fun! zoo was

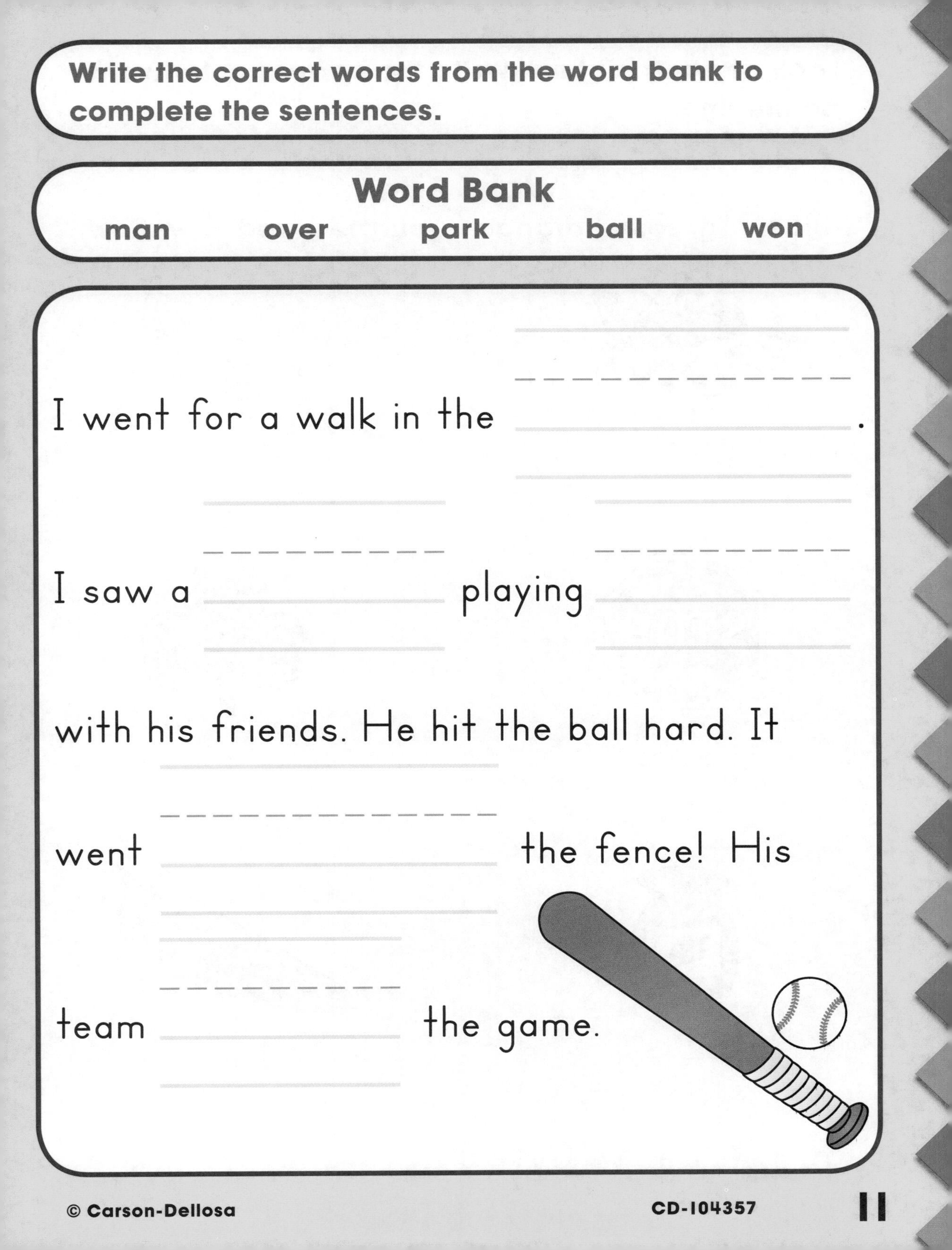

Write the correct words from the word bank to complete the sentences.

Word Bank

man over park ball won

I went for a walk in the ________.

I saw a ________ playing ________

with his friends. He hit the ball hard. It

went ________ the fence! His

team ________ the game.

Look at each picture. Write the correct color word on the line.

Word Bank

blue green orange purple red yellow

Write the correct number word next to each set.

Word Bank

eight	four	one	six	three	zero
five	nine	seven	ten	two	

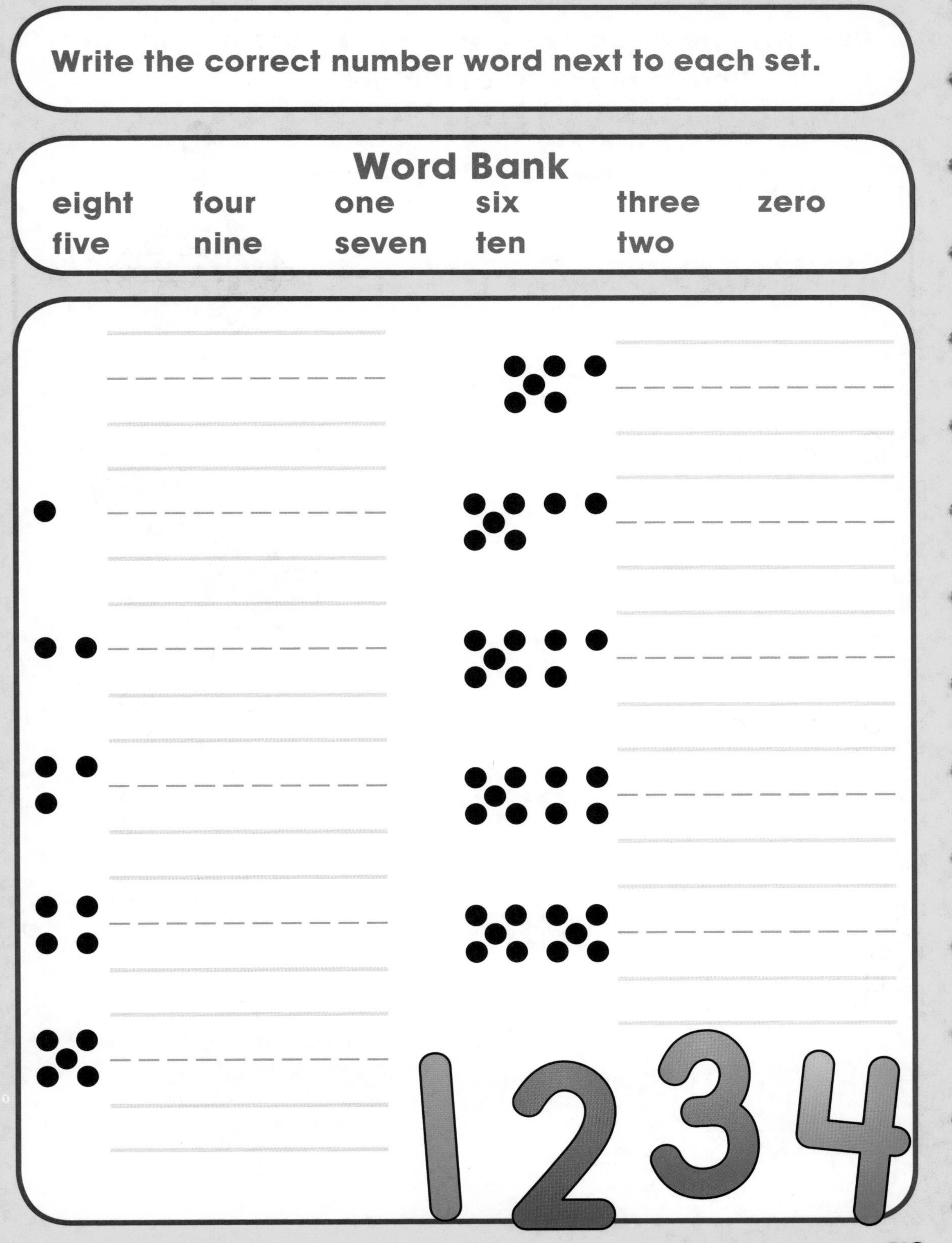

Unscramble each word. Write the word on the line. Draw a line to the correct picture.

1. gdo

2. anp

3. pto

4. cosk

Write the correct word from the word bank to complete each sentence.

Word Bank

fox hop hot log mop

1. I saw a red ________.

2. He cleaned with a ________.

3. The soup was very ________.

4. The rabbit will ________ away.

5. Put a ________ on the fire.

Write words that rhyme with **pot**. Add letters from the pot to the **-ot** ending.

Write as many words as you can with the letters on the board.

o l s p
c t r d

cot

Say the name of each picture. Write the missing letter to complete each word.

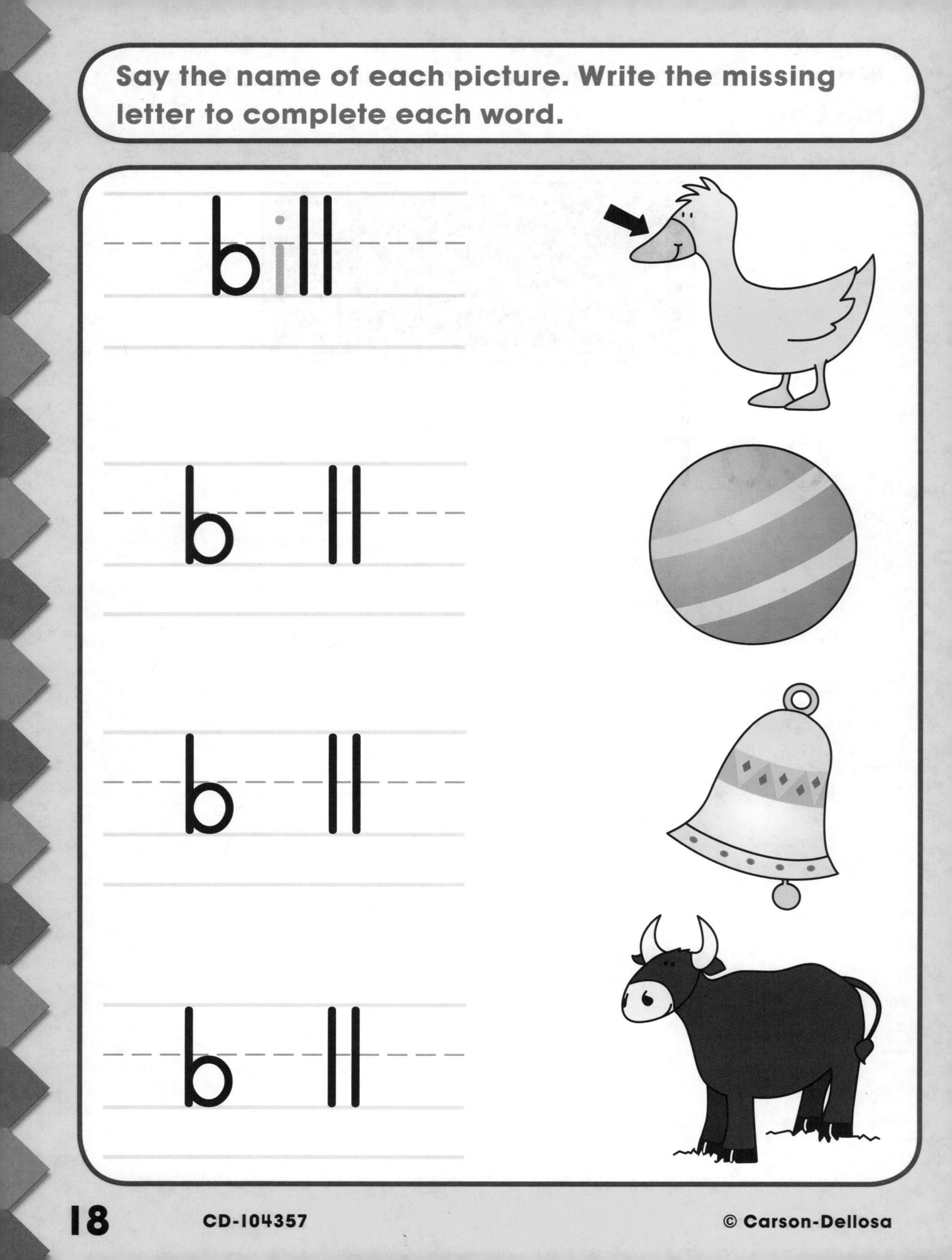

Unscramble each group of words to form a sentence. Write the sentence on the line.

1. good! That tastes

2. my That mom. is

3. see a I cake.

4. is What time it?

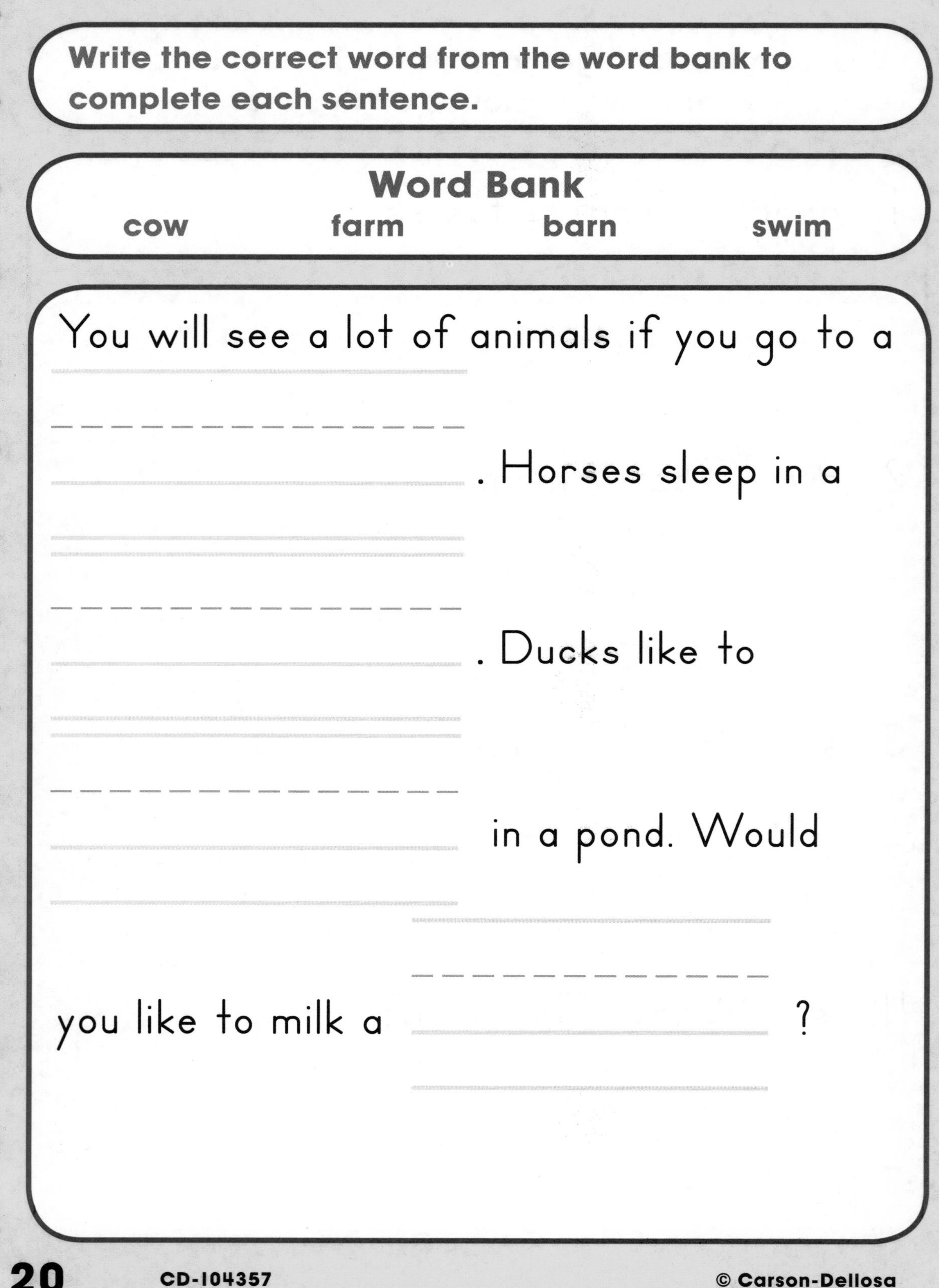

Write the correct word from the word bank to complete each sentence.

Word Bank

cow farm barn swim

You will see a lot of animals if you go to a ________. Horses sleep in a ________. Ducks like to ________ in a pond. Would you like to milk a ________?

Draw lines to connect the opposites.

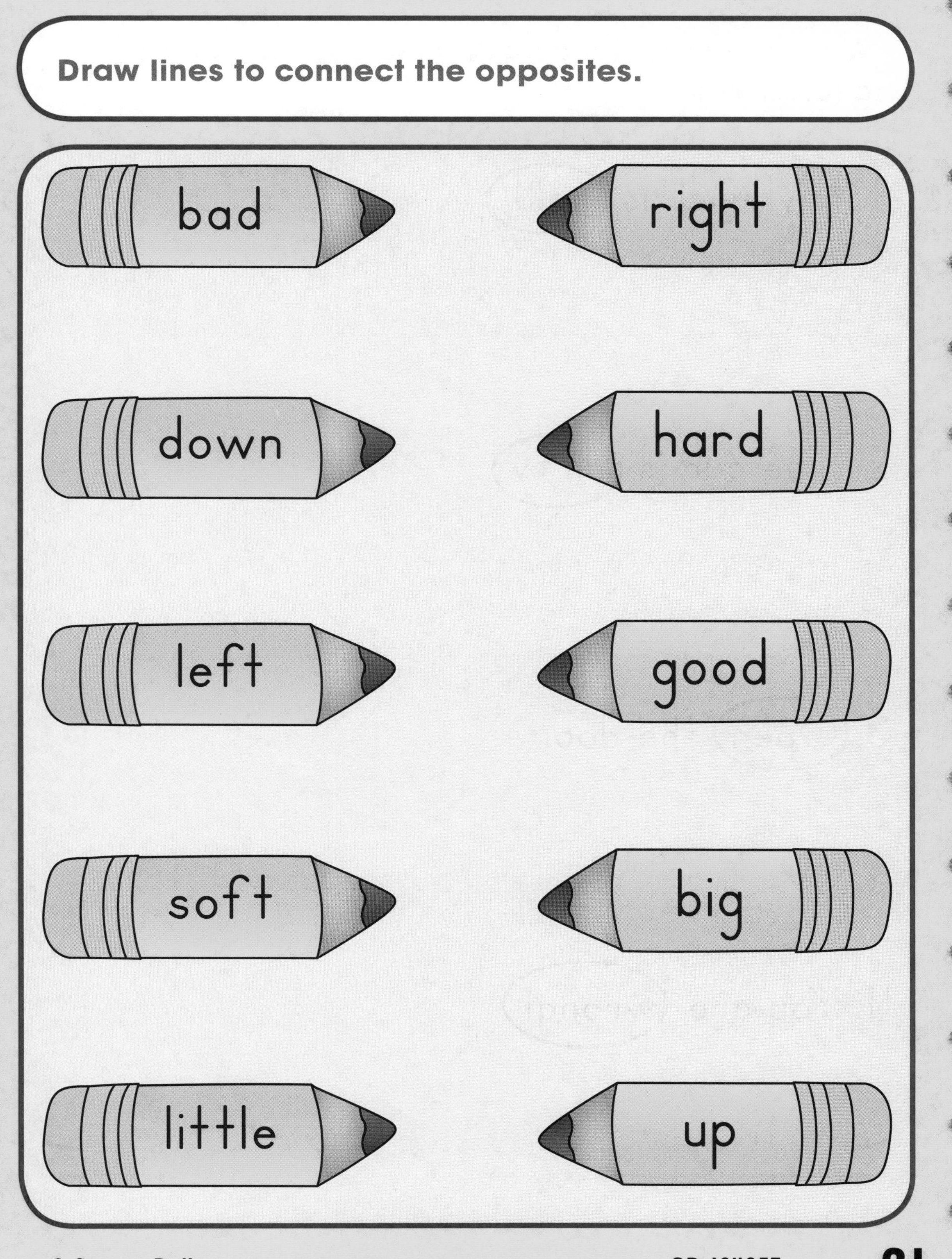

Write a new sentence using the opposite of the circled word.

1. My lunch is cold.

My lunch is hot.

2. The car is dirty.

3. Open the door.

4. You are wrong!

Write the opposite of each word from the word bank. Circle the opposites hidden in the puzzle. Words can be found across and down.

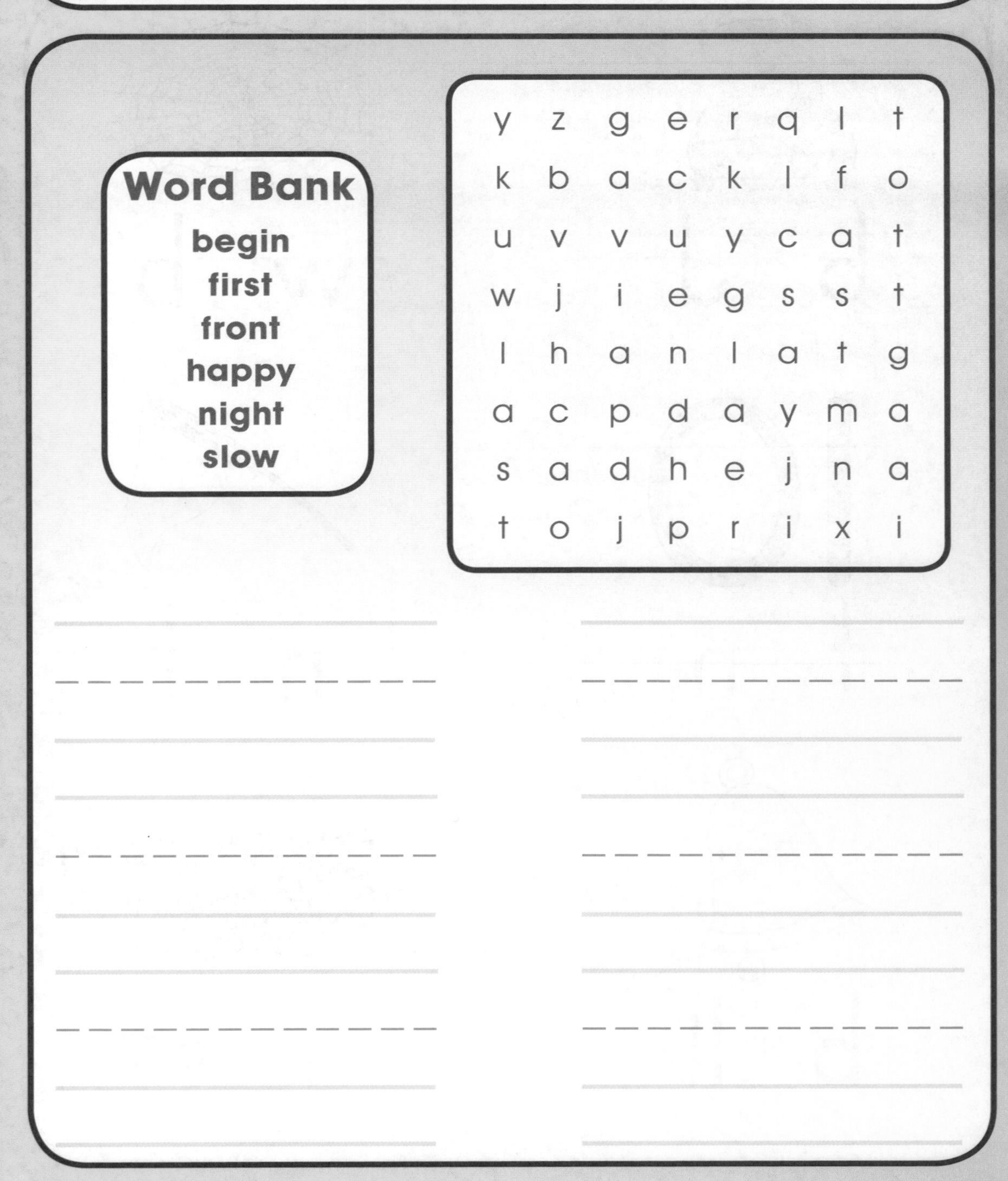

Word Bank

begin
first
front
happy
night
slow

y	z	g	e	r	q	l	t
k	b	a	c	k	l	f	o
u	v	v	u	y	c	a	t
w	j	i	e	g	s	s	t
l	h	a	n	l	a	t	g
a	c	p	d	a	y	m	a
s	a	d	h	e	j	n	a
t	o	j	p	r	i	x	i

Say the name of each picture. Write the missing letter to complete each word.

Write words that rhyme with net. Add letters from the net to the -et ending.

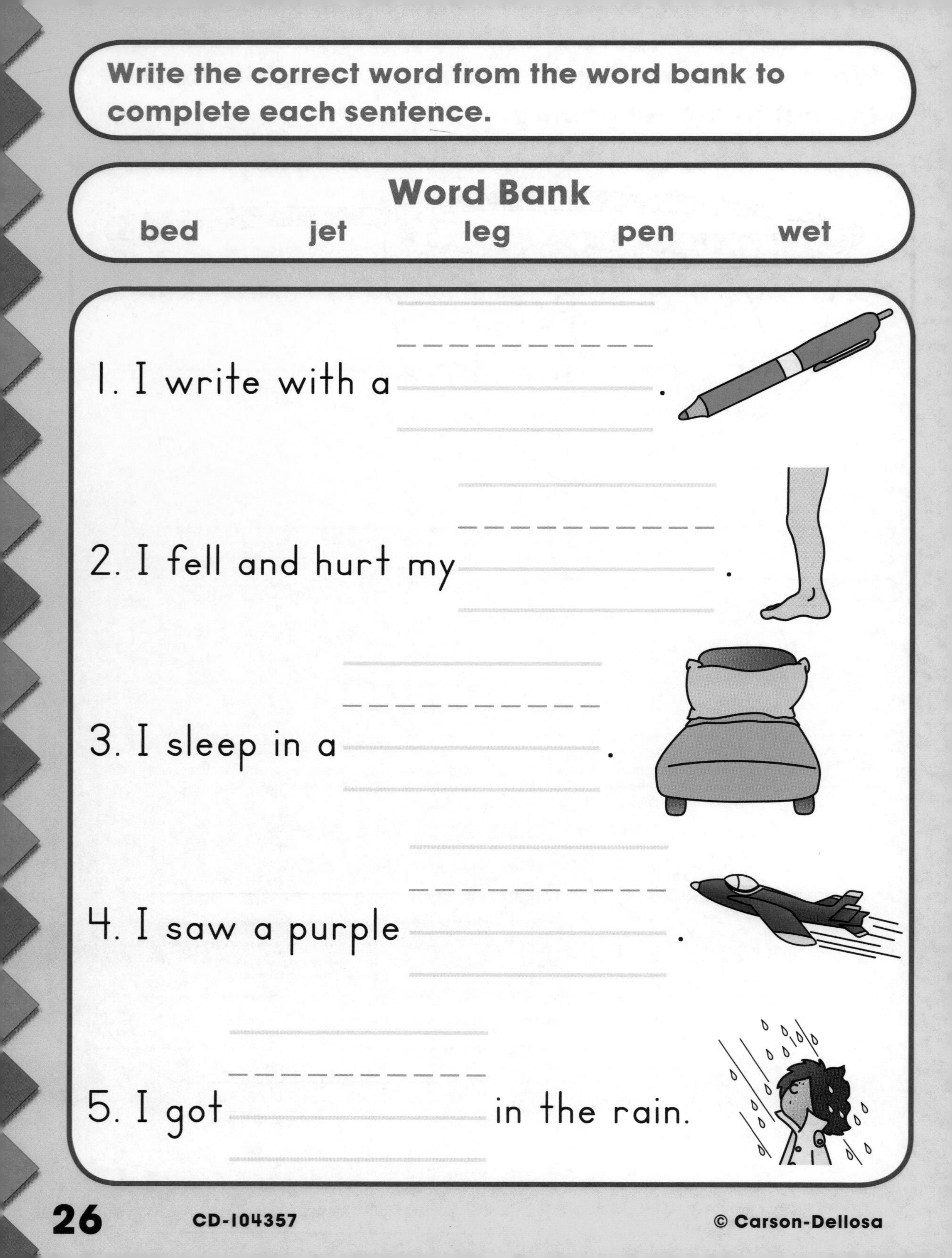

Write the correct word from the word bank to complete each sentence.

Word Bank

bed jet leg pen wet

1. I write with a ________.
2. I fell and hurt my ________.
3. I sleep in a ________.
4. I saw a purple ________.
5. I got ________ in the rain.

Write as many words as you can with the letters on the board.

Say the name of each picture. Complete the crossword puzzle.

Unscramble each word by writing the letters in ABC order.

1. g b e — beg

2. l i l h

3. p h o

4. r c y

5. t d o

6. s e t b

Say the name of each picture. Write the missing letter to complete each word.

Page 1

1. a, b, c, d, e; 2. i, j, k, l, m; 3. p, q, r, s, t; 4. v, w, x, y, z

Page 2

boy, car, friend, girl, house, school

Page 3

animal, day, jump, look, play, zoo

Page 4

From left to right and top to bottom: van, hat, tag, pan, bat

Page 5

1. ham; 2. can; 3. sad; 4. map; 5. fan

Page 6

These words should be written: rat, pat, cat, bat, sat, mat.

Page 7

These words should be written: can, fan, man, tan, van, ran.

Page 8

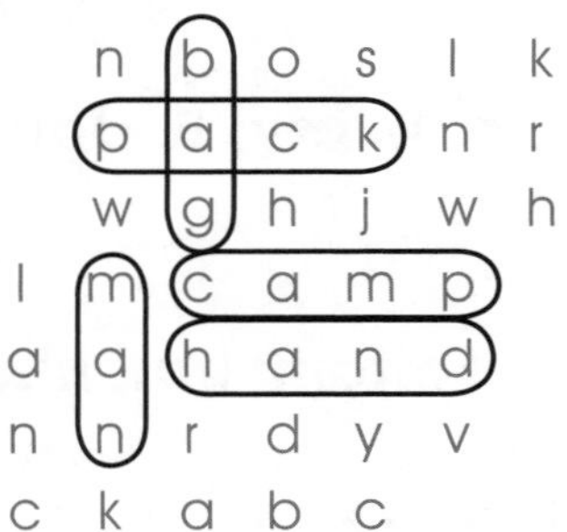

These words should be written: bag, camp, hand, man, pack.

Page 9

From top to bottom: bug, bag, big

Page 10

1. The car is red.; 2. I have a dog.; 3. Who is that girl?; 4. The zoo was fun!

Page 11

I went for a walk in the park. I saw a man playing ball with his friends. He hit the ball hard. It went over the fence! His team won the game.

Page 12

From left to right and top to bottom: blue, yellow, red, green, purple, orange

Page 13

From left to right and top to bottom: zero, six, one, seven, two, eight, three, nine, four, ten, five

Page 14

1. dog; 2. pan; 3. top; 4. sock; A line should be drawn from each word to the correct picture.

Page 15

1. fox; 2. mop; 3. hot; 4. hop; 5. log

Page 16

These words should be written: not, hot, rot, lot, cot, jot, got, dot.

Page 17

Answers will vary but may include: top, dot, lot, pot, pod, rod, cod, cord, colt, port.

Answer Key

Page 18
From top to bottom: ball, bell, bull

Page 19
1. That tastes good!; 2. That is my mom.; 3. I see a cake.; 4. What time is it?

Page 20
You will see a lot of animals if you go to a farm. Horses sleep in a barn. Ducks like to swim in a pond. Would you like to milk a cow?

Page 21
Lines should be drawn from bad to good, down to up, left to right, soft to hard, and little to big.

Page 22
2. The car is clean.; 3. Close the door.; 4. You are right!

Page 23
These words should be written: end, last, back, sad, day, fast.

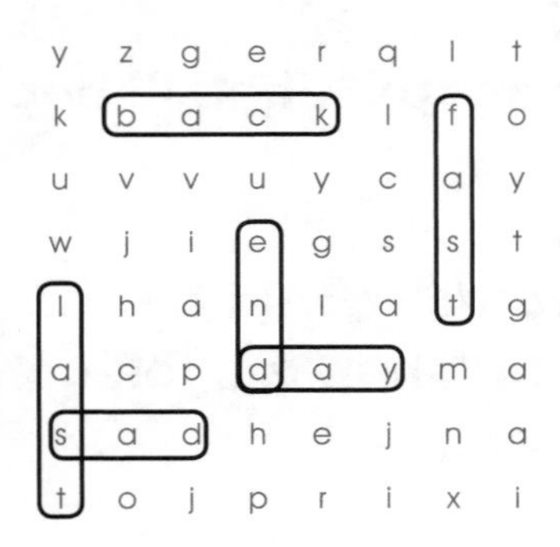

Page 24
From left to right and top to bottom: bed, web, ten, net, bell, nest

Page 25
These words should be written: yet, get, pet, jet, wet, met, set, let.

Page 26
1. pen; 2. leg; 3. bed; 4. jet; 5. wet

Page 27
Answers will vary but may include: tell, well, sell, leg, peg, get, net, bet, wet, new.

Page 28

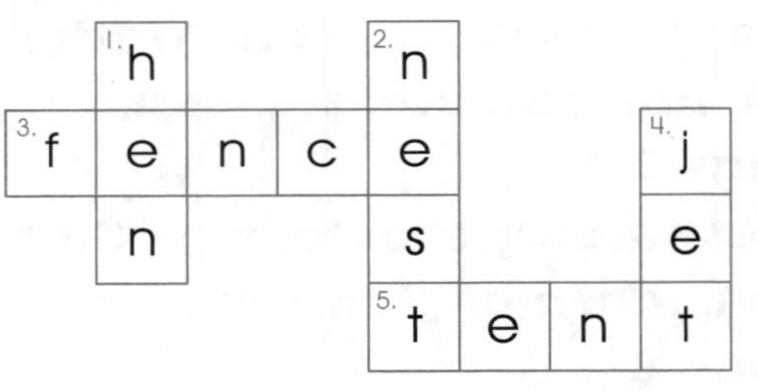

Page 29
2. hill; 3. hop; 4. cry; 5. dot; 6. best

Page 30
From top to bottom: hat, hit, hut

Page 31
1. I went to the zoo.; 2. I saw some bears.; 3. They were funny!; 4. Do you like bears?

Tear Me Out

Tear Me Out

Tear Me Out

Tear Me Out

Page 32

I have a pet cat. When I found him, he came right to me, and I picked him up. My mom said that I could keep the cat. I love my pet cat!

Page 33

1. like; 2. you; 3. have; 4. my; 5. had; 6. am

Page 34

From left to right and top to bottom: gum, bus, cub, tub, duck

Page 35

-ut: hut, cut, nut

-ug: bug, rug, hug

-un: fun, sun, run

New words will vary.

Page 36

1. Sam sat on the rug.; 2. I filled the cup.; 3. I can run fast.; 4. I cut the paper.

Page 37

1. sun; 2. jug; 3. brush; 4. jump; A line should be drawn from each word to the correct picture.

Page 38

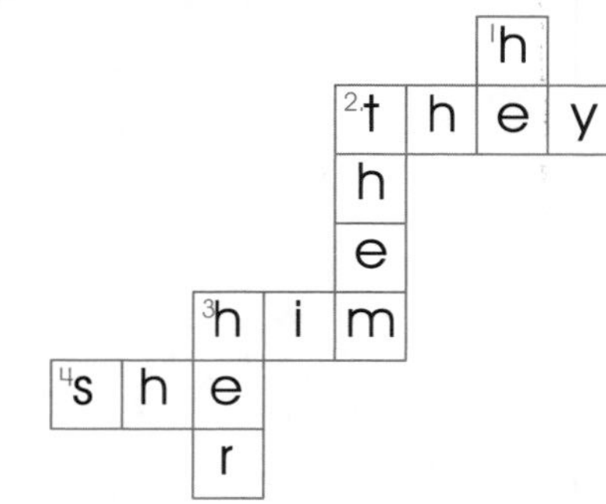

Page 39

From left to right and top to bottom: airplane, seashell, cupcake, sunflower, rainbow, mailbox

Page 40

1. My dad and I went to the store.; 2. We bought my mom some flowers.; 3. She thought that they were pretty.

Page 41

I'm going for a walk in the park. I won't need a coat because it's warm outside. My sisters can't come with me because they're too busy. I think that's sad.

Page 42

hand; nest; dog; cat

Page 43

From top to bottom: bib, pin, lip, wig

Page 44

1. hill; 2. wig; 3. fish; 4. lid; 5. six

Page 45

-ip: hip, zip, tip

-it: sit, kit, pit

-ig: big, dig, wig

New words will vary.

Page 46

Answers will vary but may include: dig, wig, bit, kit, sit, pit, tin, twig, sing, skip.

Page 47

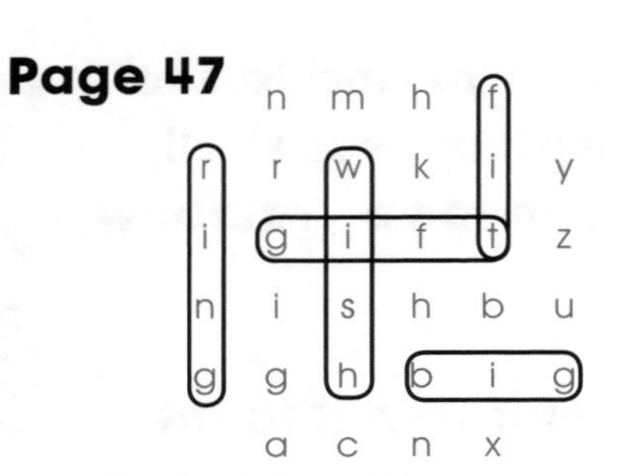

These words should be written: big, fit, gift, ring, wish.

Page 48

1. with; 2. yes; 3. were; 4. go; 5. the; 6. no

Page 49

1. Mom made a cake for my party.; 2. I eat my cake with a fork.; 3. My favorite flavor is chocolate.

Page 50

My friend called me to talk. She asked if I would go with her to the movies. I said, "Yes, I would like to go to the movies."

Page 51

From left to right and top to bottom: jump, run, walk, ride, kick, sing

Page 52

1. run; 2. jump; 3. walk; 4. ride; 5. kick

Page 53

From left to right and top to bottom: sink, fox, bed, mask

Page 54

Answers will vary.

Page 55

2. A cow can't read.; 3. A cat can't talk.; 4. I can't write with an apple.

Page 56

Questions and answers will vary.

Page 57

Questions and answers will vary.

Page 58

Stories will vary.

Page 60

Sentences will vary.

Tear Me Out

Tear Me Out

Tear Me Out

Unscramble each group of words to form a sentence. Write the sentence on the line.

1. zoo. went I to the

2. saw bears. some I

3. They funny! were

4. bears? you like Do

Write the correct words from the word bank to complete the sentences.

Word Bank

and came have said the

I ____________ a pet cat. When I found him, he ____________ right to me, ____________ I picked him up. My mom ____________ that I could keep ____________ cat. I love my pet cat!

Write the letters of each word in the correct boxes. Write the word on the line.

Word Bank

am had have like my you

1.

2.

3.

4.

5.

6.

Say the name of each picture. Write the missing letters to complete each word.

Write each word from the word bank in the correct word family. Add a new word to each list.

Word Bank

bug	fun	hut	rug	sun
cut	hug	nut	run	

-ut	-ug	-un

Write the correct word from the word bank to complete each sentence. Write the sentence on the line.

Word Bank

cup **cut** **rug** **run**

1. Sam sat on the ________.

2. I filled the ________.

3. I can ________ fast.

4. I ________ the paper.

Unscramble each word. Write the word on the line. Draw a line to the correct picture.

1. nsu

2. ujg

3. shubr

4. mujp

Write the word from the word bank that completes each sentence. Complete the crossword puzzle.

Word Bank

he **she** **her** **them** **him** **they**

Across

2. Do ______________ all have orange stripes?

3. That one is a boy. I like ______________ a lot!

4. The mother cat meows when ______________ is picked up.

Down

1. The boy looks like ______________ is friendly.

2. I would like to take all of ______________ home!

3. The mother is proud of ______________ kittens.

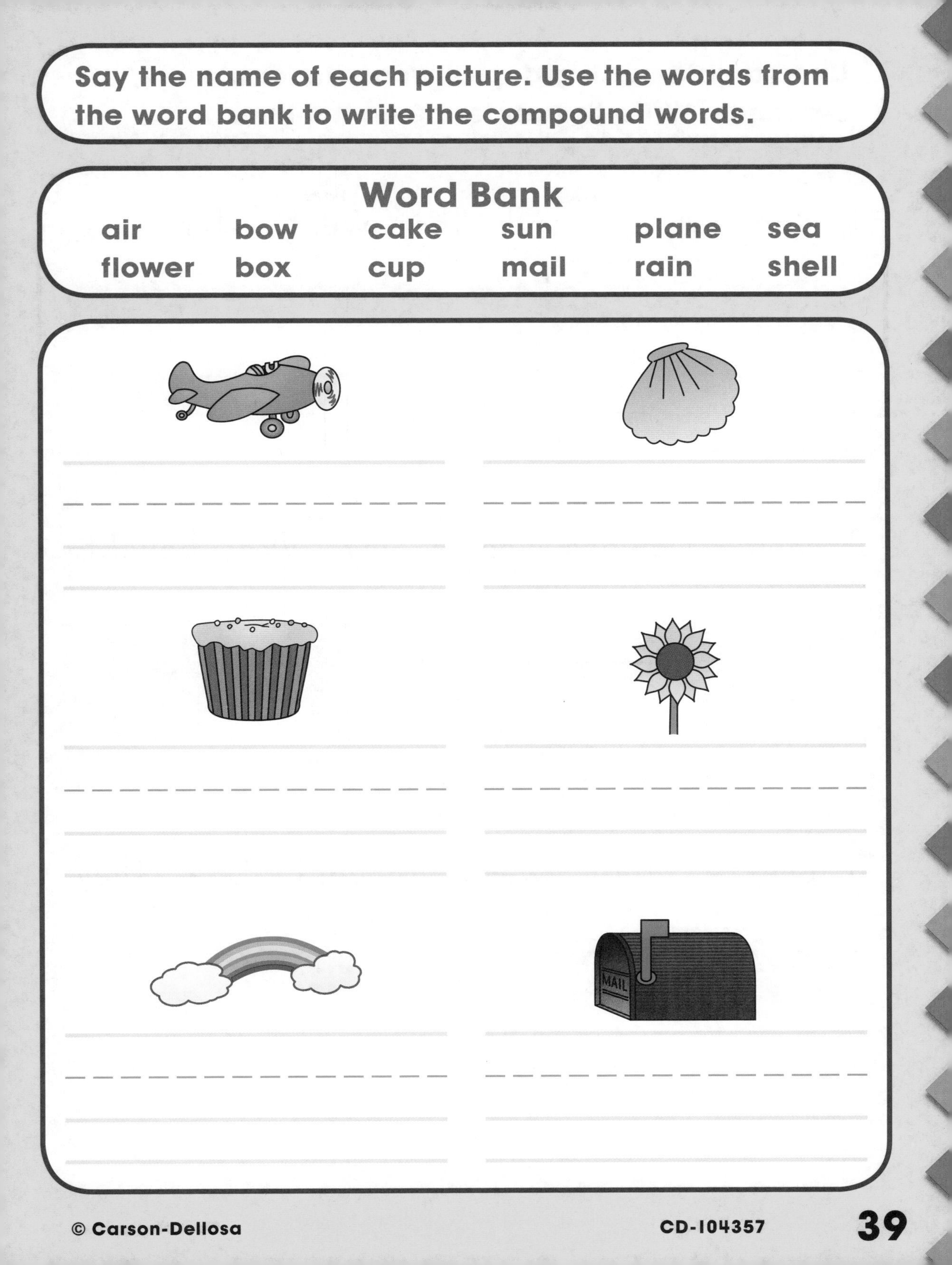

Say the name of each picture. Use the words from the word bank to write the compound words.

Word Bank

air	bow	cake	sun	plane	sea
flower	box	cup	mail	rain	shell

Unscramble each group of words to form a sentence. Write the sentence on the line.

1. dad My I and the went store. to

2. mom flowers. some my We bought

3. pretty. that were thought She they

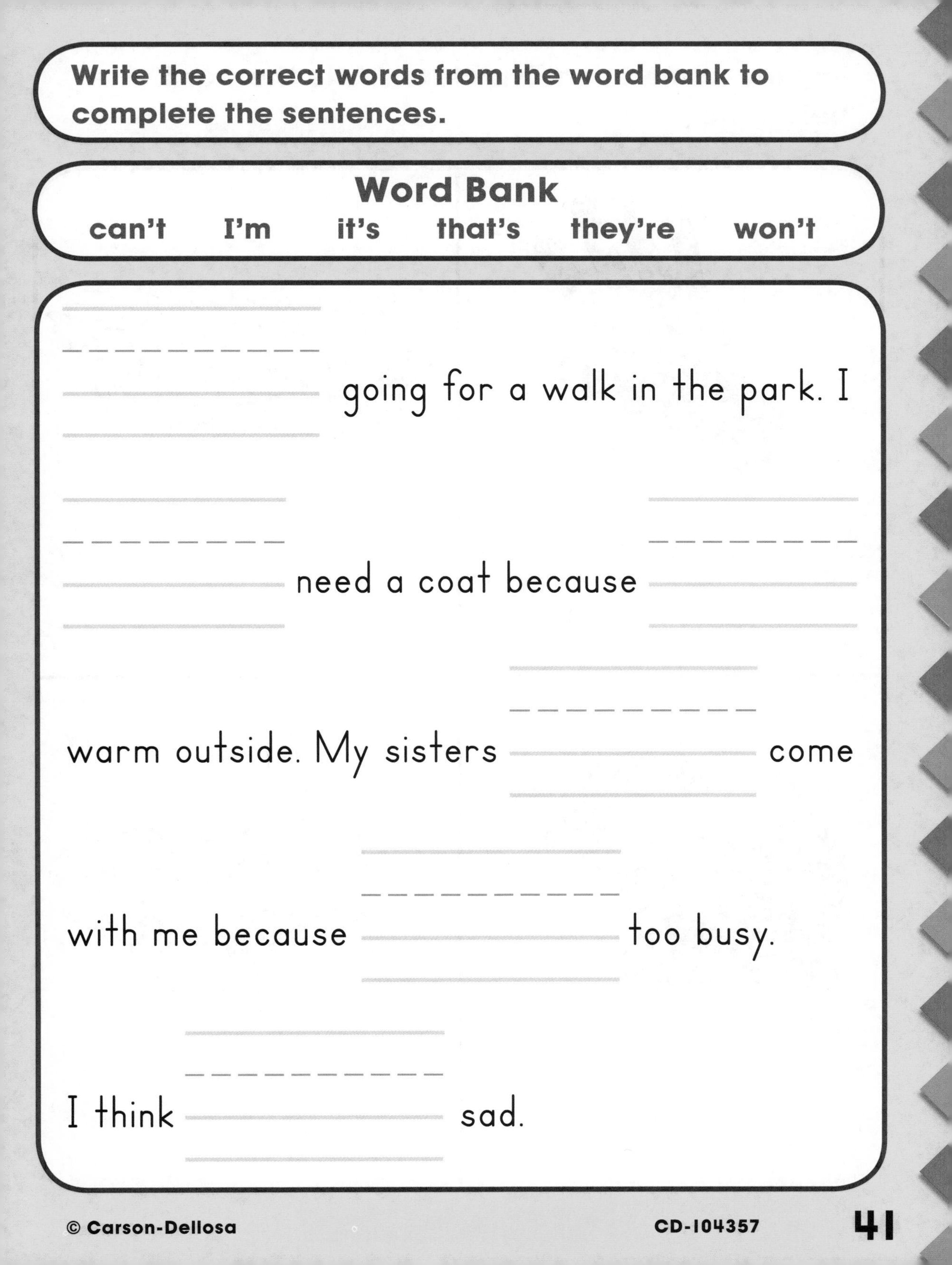

Write the correct words from the word bank to complete the sentences.

Word Bank

can't I'm it's that's they're won't

__________ going for a walk in the park. I __________ need a coat because __________ warm outside. My sisters __________ come with me because __________ too busy. I think __________ sad.

Say the name of each picture. Write the word below the picture.

Say the name of each picture. Write the missing letters to complete each word.

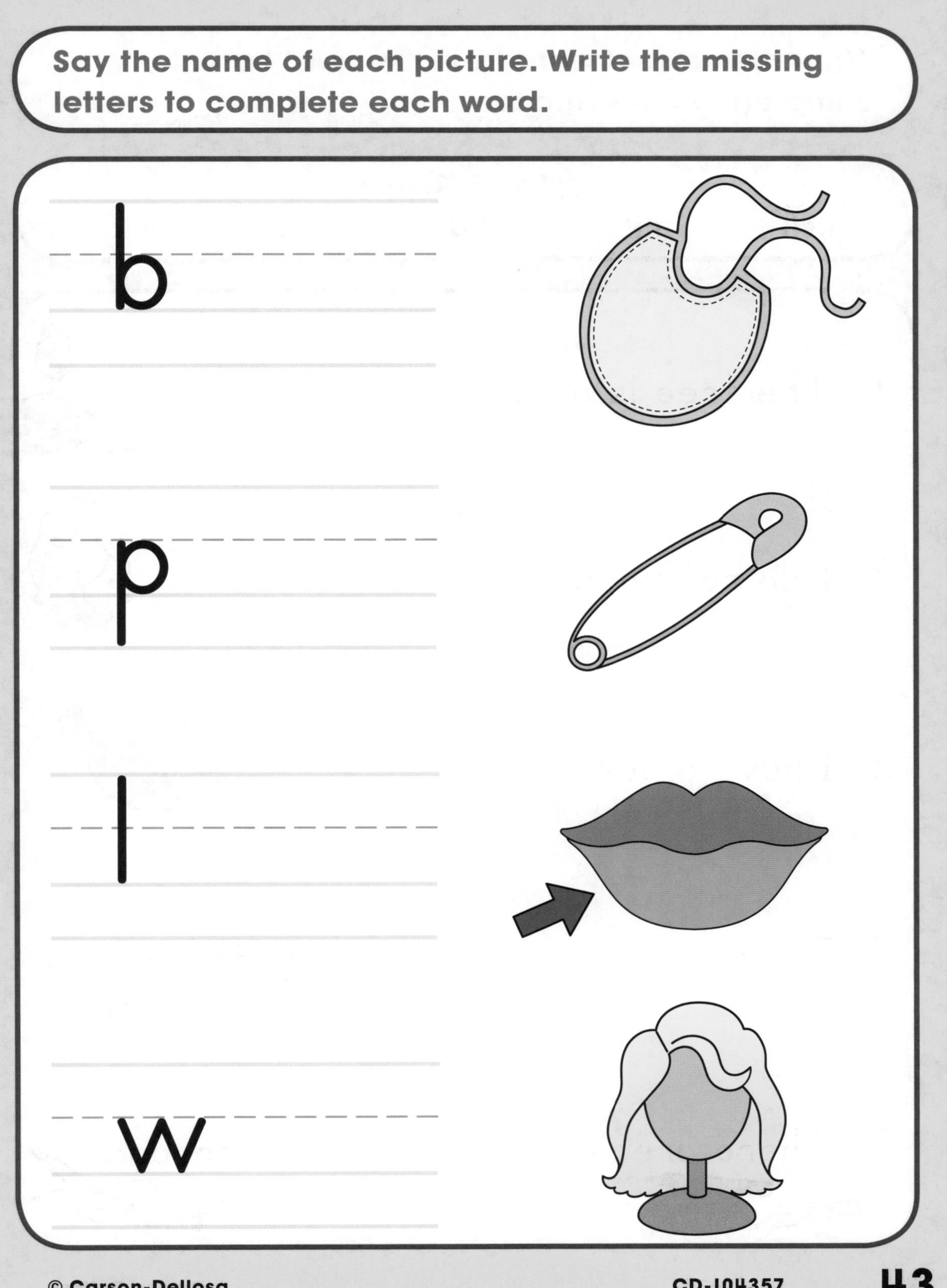

Write the correct word from the word bank to complete each sentence.

Word Bank

fish hill lid six wig

1. The tree is on a ______________.

2. I do not wear a ______________.

3. I have a pet ______________.

4. Put the ______________ on the jar.

5. There are ______________ crayons.

Write each word from the word bank in the correct word family. Add a new word to each list.

Word Bank

big	hip	wig	sit	zip
dig	kit	pit	tip	

-ip	-it	-ig

Write as many words as you can with the letters on the crayon.

Circle the words hidden in the puzzle. Words can be found across and down.

Word Bank

big
fit
gift
ring
wish

	n	m	h	f	
r	r	w	k	i	y
i	g	i	f	t	z
n	i	s	h	b	u
g	g	h	b	i	g
	a	c	n	x	

Write the words that you circled.

Write the letters of each word in the correct boxes. Write the word on the line.

Word Bank

go no the were with yes

Unscramble each group of words to form a sentence. Write the sentence on the line.

1. for cake my made Mom party. a

2. I cake with eat fork. a my

3. favorite chocolate. My is flavor

Write the correct words from the word bank to complete the sentences.

Word Bank

go like me talk with Yes

My friend called ________ to ________. She asked if I would ________ her to the movies. I said, "________, I would ________ to go to the movies."

Write the correct action word below each picture.

Word Bank

jump kick ride run sing walk

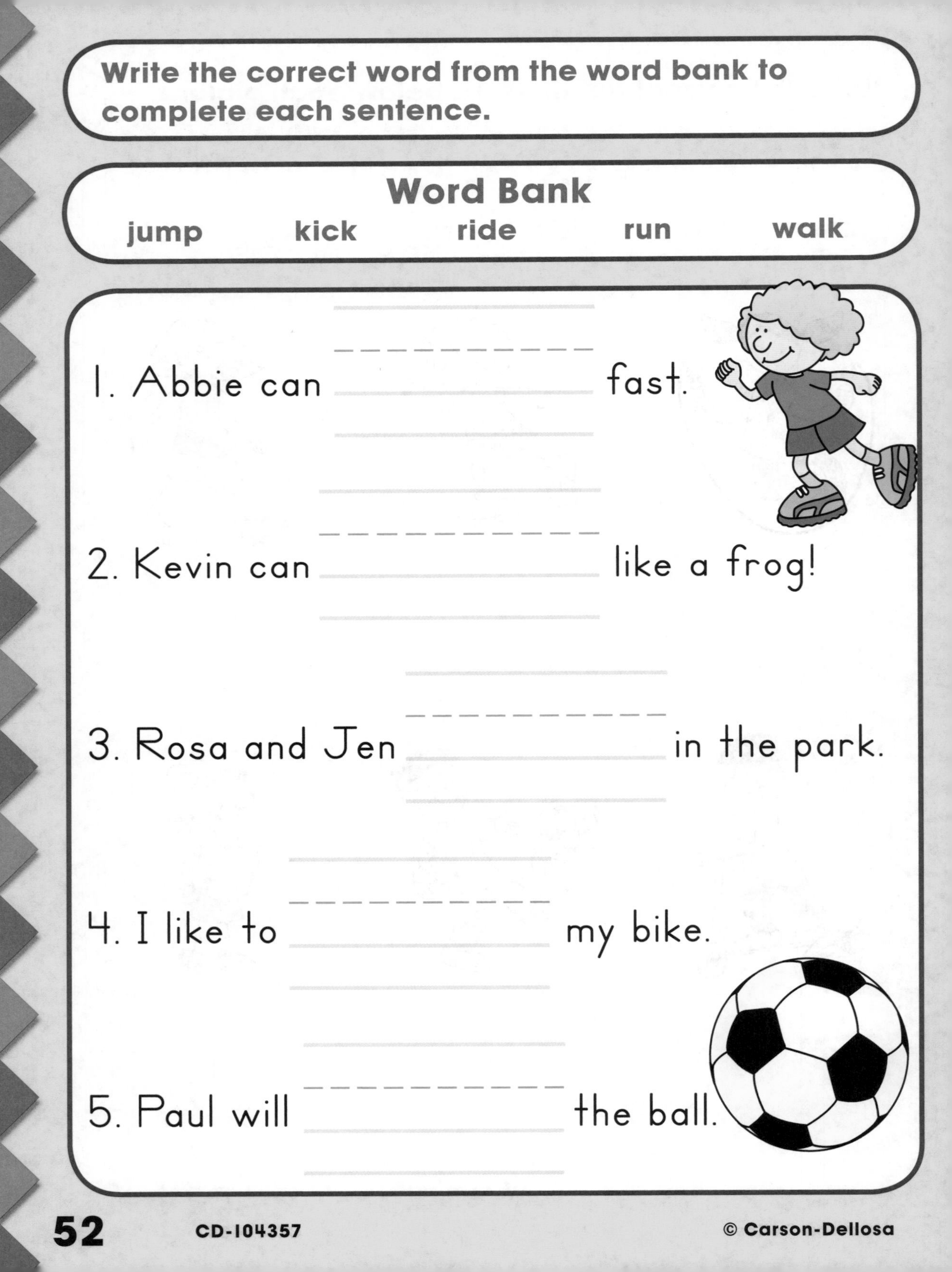

Write the correct word from the word bank to complete each sentence.

Word Bank

jump kick ride run walk

1. Abbie can ____________ fast.

2. Kevin can ____________ like a frog!

3. Rosa and Jen ____________ in the park.

4. I like to ____________ my bike.

5. Paul will ____________ the ball.

Say the name of each picture. Write the word below the picture.

Answer each question about a pretend pet. Draw the pet in the box below.

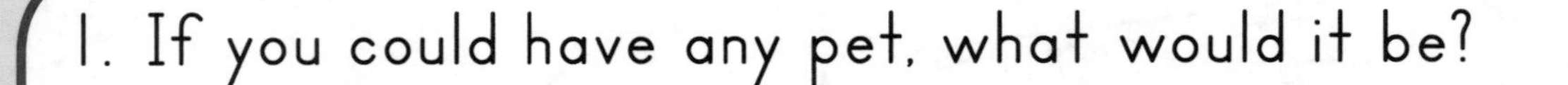

1. If you could have any pet, what would it be?

2. What would you name it?

3. Where would it sleep?

4. What would you feed it?

Write a complete sentence to answer each question.

1. Can a dog fly?

A dog can't fly.

2. Can a cow read?

3. Can a cat talk?

4. Can you write with an apple?

Look at the picture. Write a question about the picture. Write a sentence that answers your question.

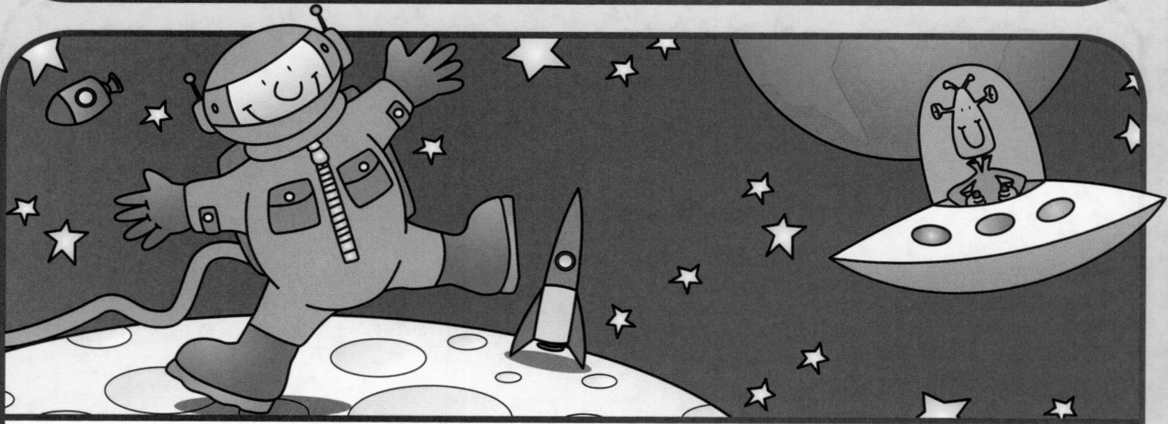

Question:

Answer:

Look at the picture. Write a question about the picture. Write a sentence that answers your question.

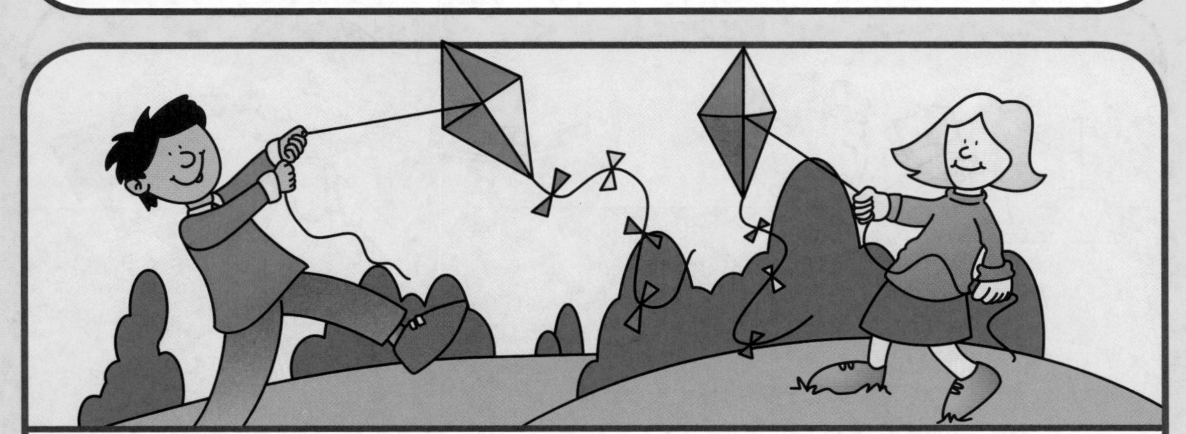

Question:

Answer:

Write a story about the picture.

Write two or three sentences that tell what you see in the picture.